THE FOUR SEASONS

A FIREFLY BOOK

Published by Firefly Books Ltd. 2006

First printing

Published in the United States by
Firefly Books (U.S.) Inc.
P.O. Box 1338, Ellicott Station
Buffalo, New York 14205

Published in Canada by
Firefly Books Ltd.
66 Leek Crescent
Richmond Hill, Ontario L4B 1H1

Created and produced in Italy by
McRae Books
Borgo Santa Croce
8 – 50122, Florence

Series Editor: Anne McRae
Illustrators: Fiammetta Dogi, Antonella Pastorelli, Manuela Cappon, Matteo Chesi, Ferruccio Cucchiarini, Paula Holguín, Studio Stalio (Alessandro Cantucci, Fabiano Fabbrucci and Andrea Morandi) and Thomas Trojer
Art Director: Marco Nardi
Editor: Anne McRae
Researcher: Christina Longman
Repro: Litocolor, Florence

Publisher Cataloging-in-Publication Data (U.S.)

Jones, Annie.
    The four seasons : uncovering nature / Annie Jones.
[52] p. : col. ill. ;   cm.
Includes index.
Summary: Illustrated guide to the seasons and their impact on plants and animals.
ISBN 1-55407-137-2
1. Seasons -- Juvenile literature.   I. Title.
508.2   dc22   QB637.4.J66 2005

Library and Archives Canada Cataloguing in Publication

Jones, Annie
    The four seasons : uncovering nature / Annie Jones.
Includes index.
ISBN 1-55407-137-2
    1. Seasons--Juvenile literature. I. Title.
QB637.4.J65 2006   j508.2   C2005-904805-0

ISBN 13: 978-1-55407-137-1

Printed in Italy

THE FOUR SEASONS

UNCOVERING NATURE

Annie Jones

Firefly Books

Winter to Spring, p. 17

Spring to Summer, p. 24

Summer to Fall, p. 34

TABLE OF CONTENTS

INTRODUCTION

The annual cycle of the seasons brings a certain degree of order to the lives of plants and animals. In spring, the lengthening of the days and rising temperatures tell animals to find a partner, mate and prepare for the arrival of their young. In this season many plants germinate and grow quickly, while others burst into bud and flower.

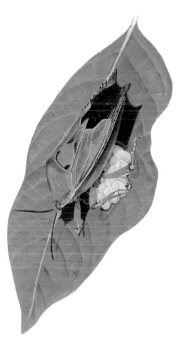

Through the summer, many animal parents are fully occupied raising their young — feeding them and teaching them how to take care of themselves. By fall, most of the spring babies are independent, but the new season, with its warning of impending winter, brings a whole new set of activities, including eating well to build up reserves of fat and stockpiling food for the cold months ahead. Some animals begin an annual migration at this time, usually moving to warmer parts, while others evade the harshness of the winter by settling down in a burrow or hollow trunk to sleep through the cold months when food is scarce. In fall, deciduous trees burst into a final flare of color before shedding their leaves. Many other plants release seeds, often in the form of fruit or cones, which are dispersed by animals or the wind, ready to begin the cycle all over again the following spring.

Why Seasons Happen

In temperate areas of the world, four distinct seasons — winter, spring, summer and fall — meld into each other as the year advances. These seasons happen because Earth is tilted as it orbits around the sun, so sometimes the temperate areas receive more sunlight and heat than at other times. At the poles, there are two seasons: for the part of the year that the North Pole is tilted toward the sun, there is a northern summer and a southern winter. Six months later, when the North Pole is tilted away, there is a northern winter and southern summer. In tropical zones near the equator, the temperature is fairly constant all year round.

The solstices

In late December, when the sun is directly over the Tropic of Capricorn (an imaginary line around the world south of the equator), the Southern Hemisphere has its summer solstice (longest day) and the Northern Hemisphere has its winter solstice (shortest day). The North Pole has 24 hours of darkness, and the South Pole 24 hours of daylight.

The four seasons

Earth rotates on its axis once every 24 hours to give us day and night, and orbits around the sun once every 365 days to give us a year. The cycle of the seasons is caused by the constant 23° tilt of the Earth's axis. This means that for six months of the year, one hemisphere always points toward the sun, and the other one always points away.

The equinoxes

When the sun is directly over the equator (an imaginary line around the center of Earth) both hemispheres have equal light. In the Southern Hemisphere, the spring equinox is in September and the fall equinox is in March. In the Northern Hemisphere, they are the other way around (spring in March, fall in September).

NORTHERN WINTER

DECEMBER

SOUTHERN SUMMER

NORTHERN SUMMER

JUNE

SOUTHERN WINTER

When the sun is directly over the Tropic of Cancer in late June, it is midsummer in the Northern Hemisphere and midwinter in the Southern Hemisphere.

SUN

NORTHERN FALL

SEPTEMBER

SOUTHERN SPRING

NORTHERN SPRING

MARCH

SOUTHERN FALL

Weather and climate

Weather can be defined as the daily and seasonal variations of many factors, including temperature, rainfall, humidity, sunshine and air pressure. By averaging out weather conditions, meteorologists can establish an area's climate. Although the weather in any given region varies from day to day and from season to season, there is almost always a cycle that is repeated year after year.

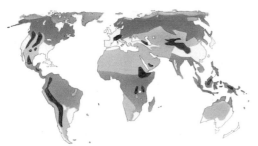

Earth can be divided into seven main climate zones. These are polar, subpolar, temperate, Mediterranean, desert, subtropical and tropical. The map above shows where these climate areas occur.

Changes in climate

The Earth's climate changes very gradually over many thousands of years. There is evidence to suggest that the climate has changed many times on our planet. For example, scientists have found fossils of tropical plants in areas that would be far too cold for them now; and about 10,000 years ago, great sheets of ice covered much of what is now the temperate zone of Europe. Most climatologists believe that we are now living through an interglacial period (between ice ages).

Seasonal weather

Each season in each climate zone brings its own special characteristics year after year. In some areas, specific weather events, such as tornadoes and monsoons, occur in particular seasons. In the southern United States, for example, the spring months of April and May bring hundreds of potentially destructive tornadoes each year.

In some parts of the world, deserts are expanding as global temperatures increase. Many people are worried that human activities are responsible for the climate change and its harmful consequences. Certain gases emitted by human-made objects limit the natural reflection of sunlight back into the atmosphere, creating higher temperatures.

A tornado is a violently rotating column of air that descends to the ground. The average tornado measures about 600 feet (200 m) across and moves at about 30 mph (50 km/h). But sometimes huge tornadoes measuring a mile (1.6 km) in diameter form and sweep across the land at speeds in excess of 70 mph (110 km/h).

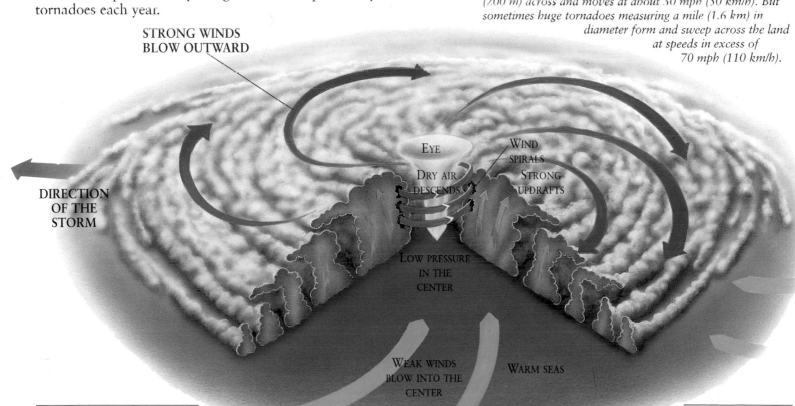

STRONG WINDS BLOW OUTWARD

EYE

WIND SPIRALS STRONG UPDRAFTS

DRY AIR DESCENDS

DIRECTION OF THE STORM

LOW PRESSURE IN THE CENTER

WEAK WINDS BLOW INTO THE CENTER

WARM SEAS

Plants Through the Year

By observing the seasonal cycle of a common plant such as an oak tree, we can see how plants react to changes in temperature and amounts of sunlight. The oak tree, like all green plants, produces its own food by means of photosynthesis. The tree has a substance called chlorophyll in its leaves. Chlorophyll reacts with sunlight to change water (absorbed through the tree's roots) and carbon dioxide (a gas in the air absorbed through the tree's leaves) into nutrients and oxygen. The oxygen is released into the air and is a precious substance for all animals, including humans, who need large quantities of it to breathe.

As temperatures rise and the days lengthen, the oak's buds burst and grow into green leaves.

Spring

Each spring, the tightly wrapped buds on the tips of the branches of deciduous trees such as the oak gradually sprout, and new bright green leaves unfurl. The tree uses nutrients in its sap (stored from the previous season in its trunk and branches) to support this growth.

Summer

In spring and summer, the tree draws up nutrient-rich water from the ground through its roots. A mature oak can absorb up to 50 gallons (230 L) of water a day. In its leaves, the water is combined with carbon dioxide from the air to make sugar (through photosynthesis). Light and heat from the sunshine provide the energy to drive this process. The tree stores its food as sap. If water is scarce, or the soil lacks nutrients, the leaves may turn yellow.

In spring, before the leaves are fully formed, flowers have formed on the tips of branches and twigs. These are pollinated by insects, animals or the wind.

If the flowers are successfully pollinated, tiny acorns begin to form during the summer months. Sometimes weevil larvae or other pests bore inside the acorns and consume them.

By late summer, clutches of green acorns are clustered over the mature tree. Oak trees have good years and bad years — sometimes they produce many more acorns than others.

Fall

In fall, the colder weather makes it harder for the tree to suck up new water from the ground. To prevent water loss from its leaves by evaporation, the tree gradually seals off the leaves and stores the water in its branches and trunk instead. As the leaves use up the last of their chlorophyll, the remaining sugars cause them to turn yellow, red and gold, and eventually they fall to the ground.

Along with leaves, the acorns also drop to the ground. If they are not eaten by animals, they sink into the soil and prepare to germinate into small oak trees the following spring.

Winter

In wintertime, the oak tree is completely bare. It's leafless branches are sometimes covered in snow, but without leaves, the weight of the snow is bearable and the tree is not damaged. Although the tree appears lifeless, if you look very closely at the tips of its branches you will see that it is covered in tiny buds, which will be ready to open as soon as spring arrives.

Following the Seasons

Animals and plants are aware of the passing seasons — many have special adaptations that allow them to live more successfully in each season. They can tell that the seasons are changing because of the increasing or decreasing amount of light, as well as through changes in temperature. These signals trigger the production of hormones, which cause the animals to behave in ways appropriate to the season. For example, in spring they know they must find a partner and mate. In fall, many know they must migrate to warmer places.

In summer, the arctic hare has a plain brown coat that blends in well with the summer landscape.

In spring and fall, the arctic hare has a speckled coat, making it hard for predators to spot it against the mixed soil and snow of its habitat.

Clever clothing

Some animals change the color of their coats according to the season. The arctic hare, for example, changes from brown in summer to speckled white and brown in the fall to pure white in winter. These changes in color help it to blend in with its environment, and make it more difficult for predators to see it.

Biological clocks

Some animals have very precise biological clocks. The arctic ground squirrel goes into hibernation on specific days in October and reemerges between April 20 to 22 every year.

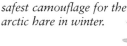

A pure white coat is the safest camouflage for the arctic hare in winter.

Hoarding water

After the rains, this spiky cactus stores as much water as it can. It swells out until it is shaped like a barrel. As the cactus gradually uses up its private water supply, it takes on its normal, thinner shape again.

A fox will sometimes invade the territory of its neighbors. Members of the opposite sex tend to be more tolerant of one another, and disputes between neighbors are usually ritualized contests, with little harm done. When a stranger of the same sex is encountered, however, fighting can be ferocious.

Territorial behavior

Badgers, foxes and wolves mark out their territories with urine, or little piles of excrement or both throughout the year. During the breeding season, scent marking becomes much more frequent. The animals patrol the boundaries of their territories, marking tree stumps, rocks and other landmarks to tell others to keep out. Scent marking helps a fox to keep track of where it has been and informs other foxes of its sex, status and individual identity. Such good communication reduces the need for conflict.

1

2

3

4

1. In spring and early summer, female monarch butterflies lay their eggs on milkweed leaves. 2. After a few days, the eggs hatch into caterpillars. The caterpillars feed on the milkweed, absorbing its toxic chemicals, which deter birds and other predators from eating them.

3 & 4. After one to six weeks, the caterpillars turn into bright green pupae, or chrysalises, which hang from milkweed leaves.

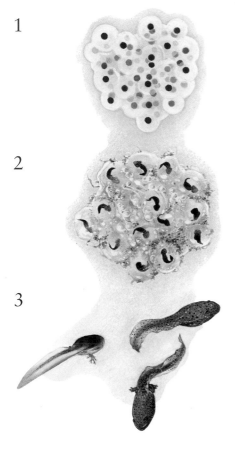

1

2

3

Metamorphosis

Metamorphosis comes from two Greek words and means a change in shape. There are two types of metamorphosis: complete and incomplete. Complete metamorphosis is said to occur when an animal passes through four distinct life stages, consisting of egg, larva, pupa (chrysalis) and adult. Incomplete metamorphosis occurs when the animal passes through three life stages: egg, nymph (or larva) and adult. The majority of insects undergo complete metamorphosis. Most amphibians go through incomplete metamorphosis, although the life stages are more pronounced in frogs and toads. A few fish, such as eels, also drastically change shape when they become adults.

Frogs and toads

Frogs and toads in temperate areas hibernate in winter and breed in the spring. The females lay their eggs in water. The eggs are either abandoned or protected by one of the adults. Eventually they hatch into larvae known as tadpoles. Like fish, tadpoles have gills and live entirely in water, mainly eating vegetation. Depending on the species, the tadpole stage can last from a few days to up to three years. Adult frogs have lungs instead of gills and spend much of the time out of the water. They are usually meat eaters.

4

1. Frogs lay hundreds of eggs (spawn) in the water.
2. The eggs hatch into tiny tadpoles.
3. The tadpoles grow and begin to take on adult features, such as hind legs.
4. The adult frog has powerful hind legs, which it uses to jump around on land. Its gills disappear, so although the frog is still at home in the water, it must come to the surface to breathe.

5

5. The chrysalis stage lasts for 9 to 15 days. About 24 hours before the butterfly hatches, the chrysalis becomes transparent.

6

6. The adult butterfly emerges completely from its chrysalis and unfolds its wings.

Monarch butterflies

The life cycle of the monarch butterfly is an example of complete metamorphosis. By late summer, the monarchs have all become adult butterflies, and are ready to undertake an incredible journey. They fly from Canada and the northern United States southward for about 1,000 miles (1,600 km) to warmer areas such as Florida, California and Mexico. The butterflies spend the winter hibernating in trees. The milkweed they ate as caterpillars still protects them against most predators. In spring, they head north again, and the females lay eggs as they go. None of the butterflies lives long enough to complete the round trip, but the next generation repeats the migration journey.

7. Adult monarchs feast on the nectar of milkweed flowers.

7

1. Yak
2. Goat antelopes
3. Markhor
4. Snow leopard
5. Cornish chough
6. Bearded vulture
7. Tibetan argali
8. Bharal
9. Bobak marmot
10. Apollo butterfly
11. Bar-headed goose
12. Himalayan tahr
13. Himalayan black bear
14. Wall creepers
15. Moupin pika

All the goat antelope species are agile climbers. Raised in the high mountains, they are sure-footed and quick, even on slippery ledges covered in snow.

A mighty barrier

With some of the tallest peaks in the world, the Himalayan Mountains are an impassable barrier for animals, people and weather systems. The plateaus of Tibet and the Gobi Desert fall in the rain shadow cast by the vast mountain chain.

Mountain animals

Above the snow line the most common animals are insects, spiders and mites, but there are also some large mammals such as snow leopards, tahr, yak, red pandas and brown and black bears. Many birds live in the Himalayas, including several species of magpie, bearded vultures, titmice and choughs.

Winter to Spring

Heavy snow falls in the Himalayan Mountains during the winter months. Many animals that live above the tree line in the alpine zone, from 10,500 to 14,500 feet (3,000 to 4,000 m), move down into the shelter of the valleys. In spring, when temperatures begin to rise and the days start to lengthen, there is a dramatic change in the landscape. The deep snow melts, creating gushing torrents that race down the mountainside. The moss and lichen lining the rocks become visible again, and junipers and rhododendrons come into early bloom.

Springtime

As soon as the snow has melted, the alpine meadows burst into colorful bloom. The skies, often clear blue during the winter, are sometimes overcast as warm air flows up the mountains to form mist and clouds around the mountain peaks.

Plant life

Temperate forests grow to about 11,000 feet (3,350 m) high. Above this is the alpine zone. Flowering plants are common and create a striking display during the short spring season. Moss and lichen grow up to about 18,000 feet (5,500 m).

Building a nest

For many species of birds, a nest is an essential item for bringing up chicks. In some species, the male bird prepares a nest even before it has a partner. When finished, the male sits on the nest and calls, inviting females to inspect his handiwork. If a female likes the nest, she may line it with wool or grass. In some bird species, such as penguins, both parents help build a nest after they have mated.

Gentoo penguins live on islands in the Antarctic Ocean. They nest inland and often have to carry grass and other building materials over long distances to the nesting colony.

Penduline tits live in eastern and southern Europe. In spring, the males attract females by weaving a hanging, globular nest.

Defeating rivals

Sometimes male animals fight each other for the right to mate with females (see pages 40–41). European hares, like the ones shown here, are usually solitary animals, but in spring the males often engage each other in energetic boxing competitions — giving rise to the expression "mad as a March hare."

Yours for life

Some deep-sea angler fish form unusual life partnerships. The females grow up to 15 times larger than the males. The tiny males have only pincerlike teeth; unable to even feed themselves, they must find a partner as soon as they have metamorphosized into adults, otherwise they will die of starvation. Once a male has located a female, he nips his teeth into her flesh and attaches himself to her. He then fertilizes her eggs and feeds off her for the rest of his life.

Courtship dances

Many animals engage in elaborate rituals and dances during courtship. One of the most amazing dancing displays is given by pairs of humpback whales. Despite their size (a fully grown male can weigh up to 35 tons), the male and female whales perform a dance together. The dance includes leaping out of the water in an elegant backward arch, then sinking gently into the waves.

During the mating season, lone male humpbacks sing to attract a partner. Their songs can last up to 10 minutes. Males may go on singing without stopping for up to 24 hours at a time.

Spring Fever

As the days become warmer and lengthen into spring, many animals begin to look for a partner and to prepare for the birth of their young. Few animals mate for life, so each year they must search for new partners. Often males will attempt to catch a female's attention by offering her gifts or building her a nest, or even by preparing a beautiful bower for her to admire! Once they are paired off, many animals begin a series of courtship rituals that can include dancing, singing or the exchange of gifts.

The Flehmen response

Many male mammals, like this bighorn sheep, have a special sensory organ in the roofs of their mouths that tells them when a female is ready to mate. When the male scents a female, he lifts his head and opens his mouth so that her scent passes over the organ. This behavior is known as the Flehmen response.

Gift giving

At mating time, male balloon flies spin silken threads into large, empty balloons that they offer to prospective partners. If the female accepts the balloon, it means she is willing to mate with him.

Bowerbirds

The males of all 18 species of bowerbirds native to New Guinea and Australia build distinctive bowers at the beginning of each breeding season to attract females. The bowers, which are about 3 feet (1 m) long, are not used as nests but as courting devices. Each species builds a differently shaped bower, but almost all decorate their bowers with brightly colored objects. The females come to admire the bowers, and if they are sufficiently impressed will consent to mate with the successful builder.

This male satin bowerbird has decorated his bower with pieces of blue plastic and feathers. After mating, the female goes off to build a nest and raise the chicks on her own.

Getting Ready

Finding or preparing a safe place to give birth or lay eggs can take some time. Some animals, like the Pacific salmon, make long journeys to spawning grounds far from where they spend the rest of their adult lives. Most birds build a nest, and some gather together in large colonies where all incubate their eggs and raise their young at the same time. In most cases, all the preparatory work is done by the females, although in a few cases, such as the Australian mallee fowl, males also prepare for the arrival of young.

Depositing eggs

A female Roman snail, like the one shown here, lays its eggs in a shallow hole in soft, damp soil, and covers them with more soil to keep them safe from predators. After about 20 to 30 days, tiny baby snails only 1/3 inches (8 mm) long emerge.

All together now

Flamingos gather together in immense flocks in the inhospitable shallows of Lake Natron, in Africa. The parent birds construct mounds of mud with hollows at the top, in which the females lay a single egg. The mounds have to be tall enough to prevent the extremely salty water from splashing the eggs.

Insect nest-builders

The female leaf-cutter bee prepares its nest — usually a tiny hole in a tree — by lining it with leaves. The bee cuts the leaves exactly to fit the nest. First it inserts one leaf, and then seals the bottom with a small disc made from a leaf. Then the bee adds a little nectar, lays an egg, and seals the chamber. This process is repeated until the nest contains 10 to 15 chambers, each holding an egg and food for the hatchling.

Silken egg sacs

The female nursery spider carries its eggs in a ball of silk attached to its fangs. Normally a fast, agile hunter, the spider becomes so weighed down by this load that it stops eating. When the eggs are ready to hatch, it cuts a hole in the silken egg sac so that the spiderlings can scramble out.

Busy fathers

The male Australian mallee fowl spends months each year constructing an incubator for its partner's eggs. First, the bird digs a hole that it fills with grass and leaves. Then it covers the hole with sandy soil, creating a special chamber for the female to lay eggs in. When the female is done, the male seals the mound. As the vegetation inside decays, it produces heat that helps to incubate the eggs.

Coming home to die

Each year, a generation of Pacific salmon leaves the ocean, returning to the upper reaches of the rivers where they were born. When they reach their birthplace, the fish mate. After scooping hollows for nests in the riverbed, the females lay thousands of eggs. The parents soon die, but many of the young salmon survive and journey to the ocean.

The fight for life

Baby cuckoos hatch into nests that were built by other birds. The female cuckoos lay their eggs in these nests then fly away, leaving another bird to incubate and care for their chicks. Often, when the cuckoo chick hatches first, it pushes the other eggs in the nest over the side so that it will have the undivided attention of its foster parents.

Froglets

Not all frogs pass through the tadpole stage (see page 12). A few species, like these South American rain frogs, develop inside their clear, jelly-like eggs and then hatch as fully formed froglets.

Tiny joeys

Kangaroo babies, known as joeys, are less than $\frac{1}{2}$ inch (1 cm) long at birth. Completely blind and having no back legs, the tiny animal crawls through its mother's stomach hair to the pouch. Inside, it finds and attaches itself to a long milk teat. The joey only emerges from the pouch after about six months.

The tiny kangaroo is attached to its mother's teat in the pouch. As the months pass the milk becomes richer in fat, helping the baby to grow.

Up and away

Herd animals of the African savanna, such as zebras and antelopes, are a favorite food of lions, cheetahs, jackals and other fierce predators. These animals are especially vulnerable when they can't run fast enough to stay with the herd, for example when they are old, sick or newborn. To avoid being eaten, the young animals wobble to their feet just a few minutes after birth, and within hours they are able to keep up with the herd.

Caring mums

Elephant mothers must wait for almost two years before their calves are born. When the moment of birth approaches the mother withdraws to a sheltered spot where she is joined by close female relatives. At birth an African elephant calf can weigh over 250 pounds (120 kg). Within an hour of birth the calf has usually been helped to its feet and is suckling its mother. Elephant calves stay with their mothers for several years. Young female elephants within the herd, known as all-mothers, often help the real mothers to look after their young.

Launching into Life

After weeks, months or even years of waiting and preparation, the baby animals are finally ready to be born. Many will hatch unattended from eggs deposited by their mothers in sheltered places. In cases where the young are not cared for by their parents typically a large number of eggs are laid, since many of the babies will be eaten by predators. However, among mammals and many bird species, the young are helpless at birth and would die without parental care.

Breaking out

Like most reptiles, leopard tortoises hatch from eggs. The female buries her eggs in a sandy spot where they will be warm and safe. After several months, when the baby tortoises are ready to hatch, they use a special "egg tooth" on their jaws to pierce their leathery egg shells. Then they use their front legs to scramble out of their eggs.

Clawing up

Hatchling hoatzins venture from their nests even before they can fly. Although they look clumsy, they have two well-developed claws on each wing that they use to cling to branches. Because the hatchlings are mobile they can avoid predators by leaving and returning to the nest as they please. They lose the wing claws when they become adults.

Spring to Summer

The temperate grasslands of southern South America, also known as the pampas, receive most of their 40 to 50 inches (1,000 to 1,250 mm) of annual rainfall in spring and early summer. At this time of year many parts of the grasslands are transformed into vast mosquito-infected marshlands. The animals that live there are well adapted to these conditions. As the season advances, the marshes gradually dry out.

Wallowing

Capybaras are the world's largest rodents. With their slightly webbed feet, they are strong swimmers and are never found far from water. Capybaras normally live together in groups of 10 to 30 individuals, but as the summer progresses and the pampas dry out, they often congregate in groups of 100 or more in the vicinity of the shrinking pools. Anteaters and toads are also well adapted to the wet pampas springs.

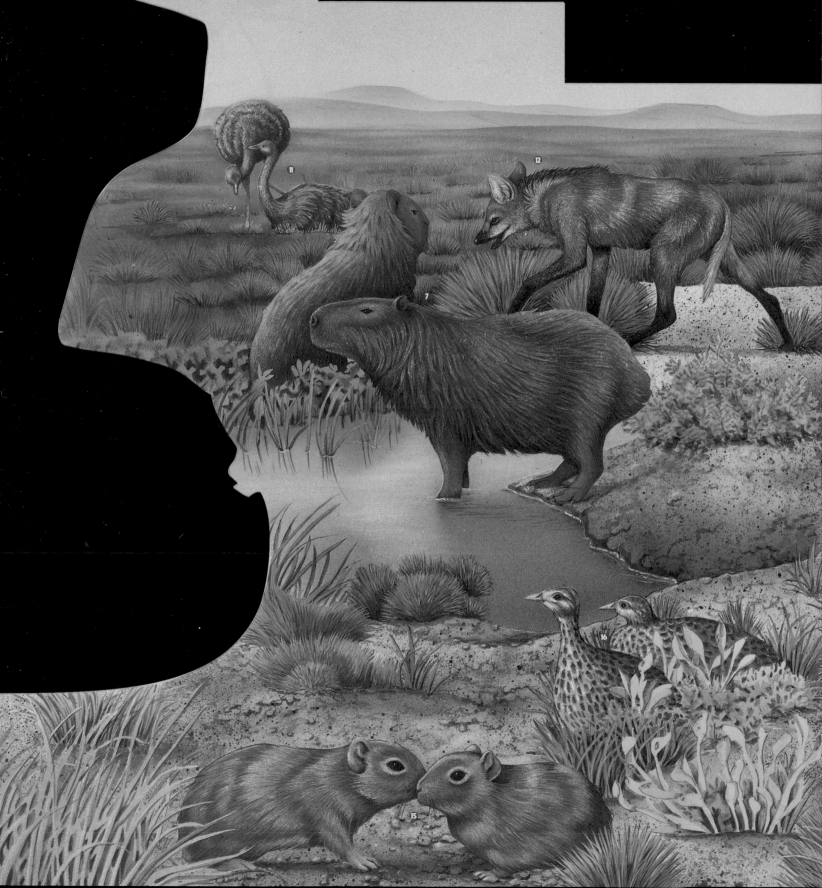

The "high sun" or dry season

By December (summertime in the Southern Hemisphere), the pampas have dried out. Frequent fires mean that few trees manage to get established. The grasses, however, are well adapted to fires and soon grow back. Strong winds blow almost continually, and most of the animals crowd around the few remaining water pools. Many live in underground burrows, sheltered from the wind, heat and fires.

Guanacos

Guanacos are wild herbivores related to llamas. Well suited to life on the South American grasslands, they can go for long periods without drinking and are also good swimmers. Females give birth in spring (August to September) every other year.

Viscachas and armadillos

Viscachas live in groups of about 20 animals, in vast underground galleries. They use the mounds of excavated soil around the entrances to their dens as lookout posts, where they watch for predators. Armadillos also dig burrows, used for resting and raising their young.

The Busy Season

By early summer, many animals have given birth or hatched their young from eggs. Now begins the busy season of caring for the young, feeding them and keeping them safe from predators. During the first few weeks of their lives, bird chicks need to be fed continually by their parents. Young mammals also need a lot of parental care, since they are often born blind and completely helpless. Many mammal mothers move their offspring frequently, so that predators will not learn where the young are hidden while the mothers are out hunting.

A female quail takes a break from its eggs. Like all ground-nesting birds, quails incubate their eggs for a long time.

A precious load

Female scorpions keep their young safe from predators by carrying them on their backs for the first six weeks of their lives. The baby scorpions absorb water through the mother's skin and feed on reserves built up before birth.

Incubating eggs

All birds lays eggs, which must be kept warm until they hatch. Almost all birds do this by sitting on their eggs, often for several weeks at a time. It is usually the female bird that incubates the eggs, although sometimes the male bird takes turns. Female birds are usually less colorful than the males, making them harder to spot as they sit on their eggs, and safer from predators.

Suckling young

All mammal mothers suckle their young on milk during the early part of their lives. The mothers need to be healthy and well fed so they can produce the milk their offspring need to thrive and grow.

Forever hungry

Many chicks have insatiable appetites. Parent birds of some species have been recorded making 900 trips a day to their nests, with their beaks loaded with insects each time. When the chicks are hungry, they open their mouths, often exposing brightly colored gapes (like those of the thrush chicks shown here). This helps the parents to know which chicks are hungry. In some species, the mother does all the feeding, while in others the father helps.

Field mice build their nests under the roots of trees or bushes. The mother field mouse spends much of its time in the nest feeding the young.

Moving cubs to keep them safe

Many mammal mothers, like this leopard, raise their young without the help of the father. To keep their offspring safe from predators, they hide them in burrows, hollow tree trunks or even up in tree branches. The females move their young often so that predators will not discover where they are hidden.

This mother snowy owl huddles its chicks beneath it, protecting them from the freezing Arctic winds.

This mother leopard holds its cub gently by the scruff of its neck while moving it.

Fighting off predators

If a predator approaches a nest, the parent birds will do everything they can to protect their chicks. A common trick involves the mother bird limping away from the nest, pretending to have a broken wing. The bird acts as a decoy, leading the predator away from the nest.

Insect mothers

Among insects, few parents take care of their eggs or young. Shield bugs are an exception. The female shield bug protects her eggs by shielding them with its body.

Protective fish

Like insects, most fish do not take care of their young. The female cichlid fish, however, holds its eggs in its mouth until they hatch. During the first few weeks of their lives, the baby fish return to the mother's mouth if danger threatens.

Keeping watch

As mammal babies grow, they begin to venture out with their parents, learning to feed themselves. The mother usually stays close by to protect them from any dangers that may await.

A wild boar grazes with its young, teaching them what to eat, while keeping an eye out for danger.

Summer School

As the summer advances, young animals grow and gradually become more independent from their parents. Many animal parents spend a lot of time and effort teaching their young how to hunt and defend themselves from predators. For most birds, the main lesson to be learned is how to fly. For predatory mammals, such as lions and leopards, hunting lessons are important. Like human children, baby animals spend a lot of time playing. This helps them develop their muscles and coordination.

Learning from mom

Some animals have special skills that they pass on to their offspring. Raccoons are reputed to wash their food before eating it. Scientists doubt that this is true — they believe that the animals are actually finding and catching aquatic prey when they dunk their paws in the water. Whatever the fact is, this young raccoon appears to be getting a lesson from its mother.

Keeping clean

Young animals need to learn how to keep themselves clean and well groomed. Birds use their beaks to clean and maintain their feathers — an activity known as preening. Water birds, like this duckling, spread an oily substance over their feathers with their beaks as they preen to make them waterproof.

Hunting skills

Like all cats, pumas are active hunters. They learn how to hunt from their mothers, who spend many hours teaching them how to track, corner and capture prey. This young puma has caught its first bird.

Communication skills

Many mother birds, like this seagull, teach their chicks to recognize their own special cries. Studies have shown that chicks learn to react to their parents' cries even before they hatch. The chicks are also taught to make recognizable calls, so they can communicate with their parents and with other birds.

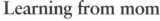

Social skills

Animals that live in groups need to get along well together. Some animal groups, including those of baboons (like the ones shown here), have complex social hierarchies. Baboons, like many apes and monkeys, engage in mutual grooming, which both removes pests and helps to establish and maintain relationships.

This young baboon is being groomed by its mother.

Play fighting

Fighting and wrestling with their brothers and sisters is a favorite pastime of young mammals. As they play and fight, the animals learn coordination and social skills, and also develop their strength.

Polar bear brothers wrestle together in play.

The big leap

Many baby birds practice flying before they step out of the nest. Like these jay chicks, they beat their wings up and down and bounce around. This helps to strengthen their muscles. If the nest is high up in a tree, the birds must be reasonably competent from the start to avoid a crash landing.

After the Rains

In tropical areas of the world the annual monsoon, or rainy season, is the most important seasonal climatic event. Many animals time the birth of their young to fit in with the spurt of plant growth and greater availability of food that the rains bring. Sometimes the rainy season is called "winter" in these parts of the world, and the conditions that follow are certainly similar to the "spring" of temperate regions. The parched soil blooms in a matter of just a few days or weeks, and animals mate and reproduce quickly before the dry season sets in.

In Australia, Sturt's desert pea bursts into flower after the rains. Its red flowers attract insects that help with pollination, but also warn predators that eating them could be dangerous.

Blooming deserts

Most of the world's deserts lie within the tropical and subtropical zones. They receive rain on a very irregular basis, so the plants and animals that live there must be able to react quickly when rain does fall. Virtually overnight, plants spring up and bloom, and animals long dormant in the sandy soils come to life, mate and reproduce.

Precision timing

The monsoon rains are not always predictable, and many animals, like these zebra finches, wait until the rains actually start before mating. That way they can be sure their young will be born at the end of the rains, when food is plentiful.

Following the rains

Every year in central Africa, at the end of the rainy season, more than 1.5 million wildebeest migrate from southeastern areas of Serengeti Park and move north into areas where grass and water are more plentiful. When the rains return and food is plentiful everywhere, the wildebeest go back to the southeastern part of the Serengeti. Scientists think that they do this because there are essential minerals in the grass in this area.

Storing water

When rainfall is scarce, plants must use it very efficiently. Some, like the baobab tree shown here, are able to store water in their trunks. In the rainy season they are massive and plump, but they gradually "slim down" as the months pass. Some other plants store water underground in their roots, where it is safe from thirsty animals.

Cheetahs use their legendary speed to corner and capture prey, often in the middle of the day, when other large predators like lions are asleep.

Wildebeest do not migrate alone. They are accompanied by about 200,000 zebras. The zebras graze the new lands first, eating the tall, coarse grasses and leaving the softer middle grasses for the wildebeest. Later, about 500,000 Thomson's gazelles arrive and eat the remaining short grasses.

These half-grown cheetah cubs have cornered a gazelle fawn. The mother cheetah looks on as they develop their hunting skills.

The fastest predators

Cheetahs live in Africa and parts of the Middle East. They can breed all year round, but are thought to mate more often just after the rainy season, perhaps because they are healthiest at that time. A litter of three to four cubs is born about 90 days later. Although the cubs are weaned at about four months, the mother cheetah keeps them with her for up to 18 months. During this time she teaches them how to hunt and take care of themselves.

Summer to Fall

Deciduous woodlands change dramatically with the seasons. In summer, the trees are covered in vivid green leaves. These turn to beautiful yellow, red and gold in the fall. As the leaves drop, they dapple the forest floor with color and enrich the soil with nutrients. Many of the animals born in the spring are already independent by fall.

1. Blue tit
2. Nuthatch
3. Red squirrel
4. Roe deer
5. Holly
6. Wood mouse
7. Sand lizard
8. Fox
9. Blackberry
10. Wild boar piglets
11. Barking deer
12. Robin
13. Weasel
14. Common shrew
15. Stagbeetle
16. Brown hare
17. Spotted flycatcher
18. Gray squirrel
19. Dormouse
20. Hedgehog
21. Badger
22. Honey mushrooms
23. Wild boar
24. Deer
25. Toad
26. Wild cat
27. Tawny owl
28. Red squirrel
29. Fly agaric
30. Mole
31. Cyclamen
32. Hazel mouse
33. Snail
34. Woodpecker
35. Jay

Spongy green moss grows over rocks, fallen logs and tree trunks. It thrives in the humid, cooler undergrowth throughout the summer. Bright green ferns grow on rotting trunks or in the ground. In the treetops and at the edge of the woods, song birds call and sing. Animals such as foxes and wild boars root through the undergrowth in search of prey or other sources of food.

Deciduous woodlands

Most deciduous, or temperate, woodlands occur in the Northern Hemisphere, in Europe, North America and Asia. Some typical deciduous trees are oak, beech, elm and birch. In fall, deciduous trees withdraw chlorophyll and sap from their leaves, which lose their green color.

Animal and plant life

The woodland floor is always fairly damp, even in summer. Plants with tender shoots and leaves grow well there and attract a wide variety of plant-eaters, including rabbits, hares and insects. In fall, when nuts and seeds fall to the forest floor, many small mammals and birds have a feast. Any food they can't eat at the time is stored away to provide nourishment during the cold winter months.

Fall is the mushroom season — in the right conditions, dozens of different species can appear overnight. Beneath the soil special enzymes in the mushrooms break down organic matter, helping woodland soils to stay fertile.

Animal pollination

Flowers that rely on animals for pollination are often very colorful or strongly perfumed. These characteristics attract the birds or insects that will carry their pollen to other plants. Not all animals can see the same colors. Birds, for example, can see red, but bees cannot, so many bird-pollinated flowers are red.

Most flowers are hermaphrodites (they have both male and female sex organs). Only a few such plants self-pollinate, however. Most are programmed not to accept pollen from their own plant. The most successful means of reproduction is cross-pollination, or the exchange of pollen from one plant to another.

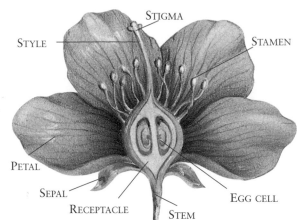

STIGMA

STYLE

STAMEN

PETAL

SEPAL

RECEPTACLE

STEM

EGG CELL

Pollination

Flowering plants rely on pollination, or the transfer of pollen from the male anther to the female stigma, for reproduction. After fertilization, seeds are formed. Most seeds are enclosed in some kind of fruit, which is designed to be carried away from the parent plant.

The honey possum of western Australia is one of only a few mammals to rely almost entirely on pollen and nectar for food. As it feeds at night on the nectar of banksia flowers, its fur picks up pollen, which it transfers to other flowers.

Flowers often have lines or spots on their petals that lead an animal to where the nectar and pollen can be found.

Flowers, Fruit and Seeds

Throughout the spring and summer, flowers bloom and are pollinated by animals such as birds and insects, or by the wind. By the fall, most flowering plants have grown seed-bearing fruit that fall to the ground or are carried away by animals, wind or water to places where a young plant will sprout and grow — usually the following spring . Among non-flowering plants, conifer trees such as pines and firs also produce pollen, which is blown to other trees so that pollination can take place. Seed-bearing cones appear about 12 months later.

Some horsetails have two stems: one with branches and leaves, and another with a conelike structure that releases spores.

Tricks of the trade

Some plants go to great lengths to attract the animals that will help to spread their pollen. The flower of the mirror orchid (left) looks like a female bee, and attracts frequent visits from male bees.

Seed dispersal

Many more seeds are produced than will ever germinate. To ensure the survival of the greatest number of seeds, plants spread them far and wide, using many different techniques. Some seeds simply drop to the ground, while others are blown by the wind. Some are encased in enticing fruit, which animals eat and then expel in far-off places. Others are released when the seed pods they develop in explode.

1. Coconuts are often carried long distances by the sea, eventually washing ashore on a distant beach, where they take root.

2. This alsomitra seed has light, transparent wings that allow it to glide far from the parent plant.

3. Pumpkins are among the largest fruits. They are packed with seeds that are spread by animals.

1.

2.

3.

Spore-bearing plants

A small minority of plants, including ferns, mosses and horsetails, do not produce pollen or seeds. Instead, they reproduce by way of dustlike spores that are carried away from the parent plant by the wind. In damp places, the spores develop into small plants quite unlike the parent plants. They have male or female sex cells on their undersides. The male cells swim across the damp surface of the plant to fertilize the female cells. The resulting plant grows into a spore-bearing adult.

Fungi

Fungi, such as mushrooms and toadstools, are not plants. They do not contain chlorophyll and so cannot perform photosynthesis to make their food. Instead, they feed by breaking down the tissues of living or dead plants and animals.

To reproduce, a fungus grows a "fruiting body," such as a mushroom. The fruiting body releases spores into the air that drift away and take root elsewhere.

King of the beach

In late winter, huge male elephant seals drag themselves ashore along the coast of California and claim a patch of the beach, which they defend from other males as they land. In spring, the females arrive and give birth to the pups they conceived the year before. A month later the females are ready to mate. For the bulls, the constant fighting is strenuous; they can only command beach space for a few years before younger rivals take over.

Fighting for Females

Animals generally mate in fall or spring, depending on the length of their gestation periods (the time it takes for a baby to grow inside its mother). Many large mammals, such as deer and wild goats, have quite long gestation periods, so courtship and mating take place in the fall (ensuring the babies will be born in the spring, when food is plentiful). In many species, males fight each other for the right to mate with females. Fights can be prolonged and vigorous (as in pronghorn sheep). In other species, like the swallow, the "fight" is just for display, since females choose the males with the longest tails.

Jaw battles

Male stag beetles use their large mandibles (jaws) to wrestle with each other at courting time. They lock their jaws together in much the same way that male deer lock antlers (hence their name).

In a fight for a harem, two red deer stags lock antlers and push against each other. If one stag begins to lose ground, it will disengage and retreat. Males generally try to avoid fights, however, because of the risk of serious injury.

By looks alone

Among swallows, the females prefer to mate with the males that have the longest tail feathers, and will choose them over shorter-tailed males. Scientists think this is because long feathers take a lot of energy to grow, so long-tailed males will make the strongest fathers.

Fighting fish

Siamese fighting fish live in slow-moving rivers and rice fields in Southeast Asia. During courtship the aggressive males circle around each other, change their brilliant colors and even bite one another. They are now a favorite aquarium fish.

Red deer roaring

From late-September to late-October, male red deer engage in roaring competitions in an attempt to gather together herds of females, or hinds. The males bellow loudly, parade up and down, and thrash at branches with their antlers. They do not always fight, although sometimes evenly matched males will lock antlers to settle a tussle. The winning males mate with the hinds, who give birth to single calves in June of the following year.

To win a harem during the annual rut, a male red deer, or stag, needs a strong body, large antlers, a loud roar and the willingness to fight.

Time to Go

Animals migrate for many different reasons. Some move closer to the equator during the winter to find relief from very cold weather. Others set off in spring to avoid excessive heat. Many travel to special breeding grounds or to areas where they know there will be plenty of food. The amazing thing about these journeys is that the animals know exactly where they are going and never get lost. In recent decades, scientists have tagged and tracked animals in an attempt to understand how they stay on course, sometimes over thousands of miles. Migrating birds probably navigate by observing the positions of the sun and the stars. They are also thought to be sensitive to Earth's magnetic field, which helps them to know where they are.

The longest journey

Arctic terns (left) hold the record for the longest migratory journeys. Each year the northern birds fly from the Arctic Circle, where they nest, south to Antarctica. After the brief southern summer they fly back to their nesting grounds in the north. The round trip is over 25,000 miles (40,000 km).

Every spring, herds of caribou — sometimes numbering many thousands of animals — migrate from the conifer forests in Alaska and Canada to the tundra of the Arctic Circle. Strung out over 150 miles (240 km), a herd can take several weeks to cross a stream. In fall, the animals journey back to the conifer forests.

Pregnant female gray whales are the first to make the annual spring migration, since they have most to benefit from the rich food in the Arctic. Other females and males follow, with mothers and calves bringing up the rear.

A whale of a journey

Every spring, the gray whales of the Pacific coast leave their breeding areas in the lagoons of Baja California and travel more than 6,000 miles (10,000 km) to their summer feeding grounds in the Arctic. The whales stay close to the coast, where thick forests of kelp (a type of seaweed) keep them safe from sharks and killer whales.

Hitching a ride

Large migrating birds such as geese (right) and swans are known to fly in jet streams (winds) that occur in the lower stratosphere. These winds allow them to fly long distances with a minimum of effort, at altitudes of about 30,000 feet (9,000 m).

Canada geese migrate northward every spring. They fly in V-formation and sometimes sleep as they skim through the sky.

Baby mountain goats, or kids, are born in early summer. They are often born on ledges and are agile climbers from a young age.

Mountain migrators

Many mountain-dwelling animals move to the shelter of the lower valleys during the harsh winter months. In spring, they head back up the slopes to graze on the fresh alpine pastures.

In single file

During the breeding season, many crustaceans — like the lobsters shown here — move from the shallow coastal waters where they usually live to deeper water where they lay their eggs. The animals walk along the sea floor in single file, forming a long procession.

Seasonal food

During the summer, conifer forests teem with insects, which attract birds such as flycatchers and warblers. In the fall, these birds migrate south. In wintertime, most insects exist as eggs, larvae and pupae, living under rocks or bark, or in the soil. They are an important source of food for the animals that stay in the forests all winter.

Adaptations

Many of the animals that stay in the conifer forests all year round feed on cones. Some have special adaptations to help them open the cones and extract the seeds within. The crossbill, for example, has a special "crossover" beak. If the population of crossbills becomes too big, large numbers leave the forests in search of food. But even after several seasons away, the birds always return.

Fall to Winter

As the long, hard winter approaches in the vast conifer forests that encircle the Northern Hemisphere, some birds, including flycatchers and warblers, fly south, while other animals, such as bears and dormice, go into hibernation. There are new arrivals in the forests, too, such as caribou and the wolves that prey on them. They come from the tundra in the north, seeking the relative warmth of the conifer forests.

In midwinter, when there are fewer insects and small birds in the forest, birds of prey such as the goshawk hunt squirrels and other small mammals.

Conifer forests

Conifer forests, also known as boreal forests or taiga, are made up of different species of pine, spruce and fir trees. All the trees are evergreens, which means they retain their needle-shaped leaves all year round. Conifer trees are cone-shaped, allowing the heavy snow to slip off their branches without breaking them.

Winter Ahead

As temperatures drop and the hours of daylight decrease, animals in temperate zones prepare for the cold months ahead. Finding food can be a major problem in winter and many animals stock up during the fall. Some gorge themselves on fruit, seeds and berries, or the animals that feed on them, building up reserves of fat. Others store the food itself by burying it or hiding it in tree trunks or under rocks.

Hedgehogs only hibernate if the weather is cold. In northern Europe they may sleep for several months each year, but in the warmer climate of North Africa, they can remain active all year round.

The big sleep

Some warm-blooded creatures, including bears, hedgehogs, badgers and many rodents (below), hibernate (sleep through the winter months). Their internal heating systems have evolved ways of dropping their body temperatures and slowing their metabolic rates so that they consume very little energy. Normally, they eat well in the summer and fall to build up reserves. Many species also store food in their dens and wake up from time to time to eat.

A winter huddle

Ladybugs help gardeners and farmers by feeding on aphids and other insect pests. Normally solitary, when winter approaches they huddle together in a sheltered place, such as under a leaf or piece of bark, and hibernate through the cold season. They do not eat at this time, but survive on fats stored in their bodies during the warm season.

Acorn woodpeckers store insects as well as acorns in their granary trees. Sometimes they drill their holes in telephone poles or buildings.

Storing food

For most of the year, Californian acorn woodpeckers feed on insects, sap, fruit and nectar. But in winter, when these food sources are scarce, they depend on acorns for survival. The birds make a "granary tree" for the nuts, drilling separate holes into the trunk for each acorn. Some granary trees have up to 50,000 holes! The woodpeckers live in large family groups and take turns at guarding their granaries.

In fall, the mountain bloomer basks in the last warm rays of the sun. When winter comes, it seeks out a sheltered spot to sleep in until spring.

Reptile hibernators

Reptiles are cold-blooded animals; their body temperatures go up and down according to the temperature of the air or water in which they live. Most reptiles live in tropical areas, where the warm conditions give them the energy to move around. In temperate zones, they bask in the summer sun to gather the heat and energy they need to hunt or feed. In winter, however, when there is not enough warmth in the sun to get them moving, they hibernate.

Ruffled feathers

Steller's sea eagle inhabits the freezing Kamchatka Peninsula on the eastern tip of Siberia and neighboring areas. The adults are large birds, weighing up to 20 pounds (9 kg) and having a wing span of 9 feet (2.8 m). In their harsh environment, they have a tough time finding food during the winter months. Many stay around Lake Kurilskoye waiting for the winter return of sockeye salmon. When driving winds and snow arrive, they ruffle up their thick feathers for extra warmth and protection.

Dormant desert dwellers

While most hibernators sleep to avoid the cold winter months, some, such as spadefoot toads, sleep through hot or dry periods when food is also scarce. Spadefoot toads live in arid areas of North America. They lie dormant in burrows in the soil until after heavy rains have fallen. Then they tunnel up to the surface to seek out food and a mate.

Coping with Extremes

Winters are long and bitterly cold in many parts of the world. Animals that do not migrate to warmer climates or hibernate have many ways of keeping themselves warm. Some, like polar bears and arctic foxes, have thick fur, while others, such as seals and whales, have layers of fat called blubber under their skins to insulate themselves from the cold. A few animals, like the Japanese macaque monkeys shown here have discovered some even more ingenious ways of keeping warm!

The long cold Arctic winters call for special protection. The arctic fox has a very thick coat of warm fur to keep out the cold. It also has small, furry ears that minimize the loss of precious body heat.

Thermal bathing

Japanese macaques live further north than any other type of monkey. Winters are harsh in northern Japan and the macaques have thick fur coats to protect them from the worst of the winter chill. But some groups of monkeys that live near hot thermal pools have also been seen enjoying a warm bath during the winter months.

Staying cool

Animals in warmer climates often have exactly the opposite problem — they need to find ways to cool down. Many of them flap their ears or tails to create a breeze and discourage insects. Others stay in burrows in the ground or in the shade and only come out at dusk when the worst of the day's heat is over.

Tough lichens

Lichens (above) are among the hardiest living things on Earth. They grow in cool, damp climates over bare rock and even thrive in Antarctica, the area around the South Pole. Here, they have been known to survive temperatures below −49°F (−45°C). Lichens are not true plants, but are the result of a partnership between an alga and a fungus. They do not have roots and require very little water to stay alive.

Elephants have sensitive skin that is easily irritated by heat and insects. During the dry season elephants bathe often, rolling in muddy waters and spraying themselves and each other with cool, soothing water.

Waiting for the right moment

Tadpole shrimp (left) live in dry areas of North America. The female lays thousands of eggs in a pool that dries out before the eggs can hatch. But the eggs can survive for months, or even years, until new rains come, filling the pool.

Index